Business Branding for the Non-Designer

A SIMPLE GUIDE TO BRAND YOUR BUSINESS LIKE A PRO

Chrissy Carpenter

Dedications

To my dad, whose never-ending support made me who I am today.

To my wife, Necole, for always believing in me, to infinity and beyond.

To my daughter, NEVER SETTLE. Work hard and chase every dream until you find what you're looking for.

Contents

1   The Truth About Branding   1

What is Branding?
Why is Branding Important?

2   The "R' Word: Research   5

Self-evaluation
Competitor Research
Know Your Audience

3   Business Basics   24

Naming Your Business
Writing Your Mission Statement

4   Brand Identity   29

Tagline
Logo Design
Putting it Together
Website Design and Usability

5   BONUS: Step-by-Step Guide to Targeted Marketing   42

6   Expanding your Reach   51

7   Creating an Outstanding Customer Experience   55

8   Keep an Eye on Your Brand   57

9   Summing it Up   60

Glossary of Marketing Terms

Worksheets

Brand Audit Questionnaire   12
Look in the Mirror   13
Get to Know the Competition   15
Target Audience Persona   20
Step-by-Step Guide to Targeted Marketing   47
BONUS: Social Media 101 Checklist   53
Customer Satisfaction Survey   59

Introduction

There's something you've really got a knack for. You've created a product that's proven to do good things. Or you're providing a service that makes the lives of others easier. Whatever it is, you've got something good going and you've started your own business... or you're ready to get one off the ground.

But just because you've got the makings of a great business doesn't mean you've got everything figured out. There are some areas where you aren't an expert. Like marketing. Don't worry, it can be your little secret. The thing is, marketing can be a challenge for both new and existing businesses. Sure, marketing may be an official word for "selling," but there's more to it. Much more. Without a thought-out marketing plan your business won't be as successful as it can be. And it all starts with your brand.

In this simple guide, we give you tools and know-how to help you create a brand that genuinely represents your business and what you're selling. You'll gain an understanding of the importance of branding, what it takes to create a brand that stands out from the crowd, how your visual elements play a huge role in your brand, and ways to wrap your branding elements into every aspect of your business.

As you'll read, we use a lot of marketing "jargon" as we move through the guide. To help you keep all of these words and terms straight, we've put them together in a handy Glossary of Marketing Terms at the end of the book.

Throughout the book, we'll reference a chiropractic business: Claire's Chiropractic in Portland, Oregon. Through each step of the branding process, we'll use Claire's business as a workable example. Here's a little background on Claire's Chiropractic: Claire has been in business for four years and things have been going great. She's decided it's time to take a close look at her approach to marketing and learn how she can improve. While Claire is already an established business owner, we've written this tutorial for both existing businesses and start-ups.

As you move through this book, if you find something particularly helpful, or have a question or two, please reach out to me. I love hearing from business owners starting out on their branding journey. And I would love to hear how this book is helping you! Email me anytime at ccarpenter@freshdezigns.com.

Let's get started.

CHAPTER 1

The Truth About Branding

What is Branding?

When you hear the term branding, what comes to mind? What does the word "brand" mean to you? Let's look at how BusinessDictionary.com defines the term branding:

Branding is the process involved in creating a unique name and image for a product in the consumer's mind, mainly through advertising campaigns with a consistent theme. Branding aims to establish a significant and differentiated presence in the market that attract and retains loyal customers.

We can break the definition into two parts: tangible and intangible.

The creation of a name and image for a product or service are the **tangible** pieces, the parts you can visually see. It's not only the product itself but a unique identifying mark (aka: a logo) that only belongs to your product or service. It's used consistently to establish recognition and identity.

But branding is so much more than the tangible elements. Brands evoke emotions: those thoughts and feelings that arise when a brand name is mentioned or a logo is seen. A strong brand creates a personality that helps consumers define who they are and how they want to live. These are the **intangible** elements of a brand.

How are those emotions established? It starts with you – the owner of your brand.

The thoughts and feelings that personify your brand are probably the reasons you started your business in the first place.

Clearly, the product (or service) itself will be the guiding factor as to the emotion – the vibe – your product will carry. A dog-walking service will evoke certain emotions, whereas, a tattoo parlor will evoke other emotions. Let's say your tattoo parlor is designed for people who have lost a loved one and your job is to memorialize those loved ones in the form of tattoos. The vibe (the brand) of your business will be different from the tattoo parlor across town in the bar district.

The thoughts and feelings that personify your brand are probably the reasons you started your business in the first place. It's your job to bring out those emotions in your staff and in all aspects of your business. From the tone you set for your customer service to how you interact online, it's all part of how you're seen in the marketplace. Every interaction tells the story of your brand.

Why is Branding Important?

Branding is all about recognition. Think about the most well-known brands. They've succeeded because their brand elements are infused into every aspect of their businesses, making them recognizable through simple images, slogans, colors, and messaging.

Branding starts at the top of an organization and trickles downward. Employees look to you for your impassioned approach and clear vision to bring the brand to life. With a clear support system and direction from the top, a brand can reach its full potential. We'll talk more about brand visuals and how to bring your brand to life later in this book.

Today's consumers identify with symbols, images and other visuals, and support those brands. It's important to create brand elements that clearly align with your targeted customer base. As we said earlier, branding is about the feelings that awaken within us. Trust is perhaps the most significant feeling we can evoke in our customers. When you can build trust throughout every interaction, you'll gain repeat business and new customers.

People love to promote their favorite brands — companies with whom they've had excellent experiences. Customer reviews and word-of-mouth marketing are huge for your brand. We know this goes both ways; people don't shy away from sharing bad experiences either. Provide excellent customer service, on top of your excellent product or service offering, and your brand will garner great respect in the marketplace.

> **People love to promote their favorite brands — companies with whom they've had excellent experiences.**

CHAPTER 2

The 'R' Word: Research

Developing your brand isn't something that happens with the snap of your fingers. It requires thought, preparation, and research. Yes, that dreaded word – research. Don't panic though. We get that most people think research is a lengthy and boring process of endless reading and note taking. That's the old school approach. Research is necessary and it really can be fun (yes, we said 'fun').

For a new business, research is how you'll discover and determine who the best audience for your product is and what their expectations are for brands in that market. Your resources are probably more limited than those of an established business, but here are the segments you can start with to gain valuable insight about your business:

> Your Family and Friends

We know what you're thinking: how could your family and friends possibly say anything less than awesome about your business? While we hope that's truly the case, when soliciting the feedback of this close-to-home group, remind them your goal is to make your business better and you need their honest feedback.

> Third-Party Opinions

Are there other opinions you might seek out? Volunteer groups, committees you sit on, parents, non-profit organizations...anyone and everyone your business has any experience with is worthy of fetching an opinion.

If you're a small business who has been at it a while, the first place to begin your research is to find out what people currently think about your business. What people? It's easy. There are all sorts of folks who've had exposure to your business. Start with the two segments listed above and also take advantage of these:

PRO TIP:

Market Research is a fantastic investment but not all start-ups and small businesses can afford a professional market research agency. If you have a little cash, but not enough to hire a pro, look into the Audience feature in the online survey platform Survey Monkey.

> Other Businesses

Whether you have a storefront or not, there are other businesses you interact with, both directly and indirectly. No doubt you hope business owners, colleagues, and partners view you as professional, capable, and all the other warm fuzzy feelings you try to impart, but that may not be the case. Find out by contacting them directly!

> Your Employees

Here's a group of people who are closest to your business. Your staff has a vested interest in the success of the business and they interact with customers from a different vantage point. Garnering their input is key to helping you build upon your business's strengths and make sound improvements.

> Your Customers (current and past)

Ding, ding, ding — this is a biggie! The opinions your customers hold about your business are exactly what you need in order to learn what you're doing well and what you need to improve upon.

Does the service you deliver align with your customers' expectations?

Does the rapport you have with customers align with the vibe you aim to convey? Understanding what your customers think and what they want is of utmost value to your brand.

The perception these different groups have of your business will be helpful in developing your brand.

How do you reach all these different groups? Luckily, there's the internet!

> **PRO TIP:**
>
> If you already use an email service provider (MailChimp, Mad Mimi, Constant Contact, etc.), they may offer survey capabilities as part of their services. It will help you get your survey out the door sooner because they'll have your current contact distribution list in one place. If you don't use an email service, try a free service like SurveyMonkey.com.

While there's nothing wrong with old-fashioned paper and pencil surveys (some people still do prefer these), there are a number of great online survey platforms that make polling a group of people practically effortless.

Use the **Brand Audit Questionnaire** on page 12 to get you started.

Self-evaluation

Mirror, mirror on the wall. Who's the fairest of them all? You are, of course. At least that's the goal. We're not talking about vanity here. We're talking about your business. You want your business to be the shining star in your marketplace — the fairest of them all.

How do you become the fairest of them all? Do a little self-evaluation using the **Look in The Mirror Worksheet** on page 13.

First, think about all of the words that describe what your business offers, how you *want* to be perceived and how you *think* you are perceived and write them down. Be honest with yourself. Think back to interactions you've had with your customers: the good, the bad, and even the ugly. Use those experiences and jot down what you can (and have) done to overcome obstacles to achieve that golden status of being the fairest of them all.

Competitor Research

Wouldn't it be swell if you were the only business who offered your service or sold your product in your area? Unless you live in a pretty small town, chances are you have competition.

You know that competition is a good thing. It pushes you to improve. It helps to avert complacency. **Competition helps you best meet the needs of your target audience**. But to have a bigger slice of the market share in your niche, you've got to be that much better than your competitors.

A mission critical component of your research is knowing your competitors. And good news, analyzing your competitors just got easier. Use the **Get to Know the Competition Worksheets** on pages 15-17 to effectively research your market.

Who sells the same or similar products and services as you? Who targets the same demographic? Jot down everything you know about each of them on your worksheets. Check out online reviews. Ask friends and neighbors. You can even feel out your customers for their attitude about competitors.

Remember this: Your competitors have strengths and weaknesses, just like you do. As you're evaluating them, don't solely name the things you're better at, look for what they do well. This is a great learning exercise in helping you truly differentiate yourself from all the others. And that may mean adjusting how you do business.

> **Your competitors have strengths and weaknesses, just like you do.**

...research of your audience's expectations will give you straightforward answers that help you fine-tune your current offering and even give insight on ideas for the future that you've not yet considered.

Know Your Audience

Knowing your audience: it's on page one of the Marketing 101 textbook because it's really that important. Without defining a target audience, you're squelching your chance at ultimate success.

When thinking about your ideal customer, you need to understand who *needs* your product or service. What's the size of this audience? Are there enough people who know about your business that you can be profitable? If you struggle to answer yes, it's time to re-evaluate your audience, expand who you can sell to, and figure out how you can reach them. Here's a guide to help you through the process:

> Establish your ideal target audience

Think about your product or service offering. Who is it designed for? Who can benefit from it? While there is likely more than one single demographic suited for your product, there is also likely one very distinct group whose problem your goods can solve.

How do you figure out who this target group is? Through research, surveys and interviews.

Revisit the questions above:

Who is your product designed for?

Who can benefit from it?

With your initial answers to those questions in hand, ask those people what they expect from brands in your market. Chances are you have a connection to this demographic that compelled you to start your business, so finding people should be fairly easy. Make their visit with you worth their time: buy them lunch or give them a generous discount.

This direct consumer research of your audience's expectations will give you straightforward answers that help you fine-tune your current offering and even give insight on ideas for the future that you've not yet considered.

Not sure what to ask them? Use the **Target Audience Persona Worksheet** on page 20 for basic questions on identifying your target audience.

> Bring your customers to life

Target Audience Personas are fictional, generalized representations of your customers. Giving each Persona a visual likeness will help you bring them to life and affirm your optimal target audience groups. With these visual representations in hand, you'll be better able to write messaging that appeals to each group's wants and needs.

Your first target audience will be the people you initially interviewed.

They're the group you will outline on the **Target Audience Persona Worksheet.** Complete the worksheet as fully as you can using the information collected in your interviews. Do you have an answer for every question? If not, you may consider conducting online surveys before moving forward.

Give your Persona a name, like: Business Administrator Ava, Industrial Engineer Ian, or Jewel Inspector Jaicee. Add a photograph of a person to your Persona. These personal details will help you fully envision the Persona as a real customer.

> Start small

Don't get overwhelmed; start with one demographic for now. Only when you've buttoned down your primary target demographic should you consider completing another worksheet to identify a secondary target group. You'll gain further reach by identifying multiple groups you can market to, but start small and build from there.

Our business owner, Claire, uncovered the top two demographics for her business during her research:

1. **women in their forties**
2. **male athletes**

These diverse groups both have an interest in the service Claire sells.

Through every step of the process, keep in mind: research and brand development isn't a "one and done" process. Like your business, your brand (or brands) will evolve over time. Your audience will grow. To keep up with changes in consumer behaviors, your relevance in the market should always be on your mind. Brand assessment should be repeated as demographics change and new competition enters the market.

Brand Audit Questionnaire

As a business owner, it's important to learn how others feel and what they think about your business. Use this Brand Audit Questionnaire to gather insights into the impression your business and brand has made on others.

What was your first impression of this business?

What do you think is the mission of the business?

What makes this business stand out for you personally?

What are the strengths of this business?

What are the weaknesses of this business? Every business is bound to have them. (Be honest!)

Who do you think is this business's target customer?

Who will find the business's products and services useful?

Do you trust this business? Why or why not?

Optional

Your name: _____

Relationship to the business: _____

Look in the Mirror

This worksheet will help you examine your internal desires for your business's image. Use that knowledge to be fairer than the competition.

How do you want your business to be perceived?

If you're being totally honest with yourself, how do you think your business is perceived by others?

What problems does your product or service solve for your clientele?

Every business faces obstacles. What are yours? And how have you overcome those you've encountered?

What are the most important notes from above?

1. _____
2. _____
3. _____
4. _____
5. _____
6. _____
7. _____
8. _____

Which of these notes separate you from your competitors?

Look in the Mirror

This worksheet will help you examine your internal desires for your business's image. Use that knowledge to be fairer than the competition.

How do you want your business to be perceived?

I want people in my office to feel like they are part of a community. I want to be perceived as knowledgeable, compassionate and trustworthy.

If you're being totally honest with yourself, how do you think your business is perceived by others?

Currently, we are lacking the community aspect. We are perceived as a medical office you visit when you are in pain.

What problems does your product or service solve for your clientele?

Chiropractic care, massage, weight loss coaching.

Every business faces obstacles. What are yours? And how have you overcome those you've encountered?

Our customers weren't aware of the other services we sell, so they only returned when they were in pain. We've begun promoting the services with our current clients to start forming a community.

What are the most important notes from above?

1. _____ community _____
2. _____ compassionate _____
3. _____ trustworthy _____
4. _____ objective _____
5. _____
6. _____
7. _____
8. _____

Which of these notes separate you from your competitors?

If we are able to create the community feel that I am aiming for, I feel that we will be miles ahead.

Get to Know the Competition

1. Go to Google.

2. Enter the keyword that most closely relates to your business into the search bar (for example: "window tinting" "Chinese restaurant" or "chiropractor").

3. Review the search engine results page (called SERPs). On the **Get to Know the Competition Worksheet** write down the top five companies and their website URLs. Ignore any **paid** or **sponsored** ads – they'll be listed at the top and on the right side.

4. Are there local competitors you know of that do not show in the top five? Add them to the list, too. Use this approach to analyze your local competitors, as well, even if they don't have a website.

5. **Review and take notes**. Look through each website. Jot down what you like and dislike about the website in the notes space provided.

    Then, use the space on Page 2 of the **Get to Know the Competition Worksheet** to write down things they may be doing that you'd like to do. What are they doing that you vow never to do? What aren't they doing that you can do, but don't? What are they doing that you do differently?

Get to Know the Competition / Page 1

Competitor Name

Competitor Website URL

1. _____

Notes: _____

2. _____

Notes: _____

3. _____

Notes: _____

4. _____

Notes: _____

5. _____

Notes: _____

6. _____

Notes: _____

7. _____

Notes: _____

Get to Know the Competition / Page 2

Use this space to write down things that your competitors may be doing that you'd like to do. What are they doing that you vow never to do? What aren't they doing that you can do, but don't? What are they doing that you do differently?

Get to Know the Competition / Page 1

Competitor Name   Competitor Website URL

1. LH Chiropractic   www.lhchiro.com
Notes: website does not work on mobile

2. North Portland Clinic   www.northpclinic.com
Notes: Site has broken links. Site not maintained.

3. Horatio Chiropractic   www.horatiochiropportland.com
Notes: Lots of info on site like videos and events.

4. Shephard Wellness   www.shephardwellness.com
Notes: Not easy to navigate. Cheesy graphics.

5. Kellson Chiropractic   www.kellsonchiro.com
Notes: Well put together site. Lots of photos. Testimonials page is nice.

6. Dr. Thomas Chiro   www.drthomaschiro.com
Notes: Doesn't draw me in. Too much text.

7. West Portland Clinic   www.westportlandclinic.com
Notes: Older website. Too much text.

GET TO KNOW THE COMPETITION

Get to Know the Competition / Page 2

Use this space to write down things that your competitors may be doing that you'd like to do. What are they doing that you vow never to do? What aren't they doing that you can do, but don't? What are they doing that you do differently?

Want to use videos and events.

Use more photos and images throughout site.

Like use of testimonials.

Most competitors are doing a lot of therapies and emphasize care after auto injuries and sports injuries.

Target Audience Persona

Personal Info

Age: _____

Gender: _____

Marital Status: _____

Ages of Children, if any:

_____

Location: _____

Level of Education:

_____

Occupation:

_____

Annual Income:

_____

Likes: _____

_____

_____

Dislikes: _____

_____

_____

Challenges: _____

_____

_____

Role in the Purchase Process:

_____

_____

_____

_____

Goals: _____

_____

_____

_____

Values: _____

_____

_____

Words and ideas appeal
to this persona: _____

_____

_____

Name

_____

Buying Habits

Shopping by percentage

In-store: _____ Online: ____

Favorite places to buy: _____

_____

How often do they buy: _____

_____

Relies on customer reviews:

Yes ☐   No ☐

Sources of Info

Books/Magazines: _____

_____

_____

Blogs: _____

_____

_____

Websites: _____

_____

_____

_____

Television & Other Media:

_____

_____

Associations: _____

_____

Social Media Use

Favorite social media
platforms: _____

_____

_____

Frequency of social media
use: _____

Uses social media to shape
buying decisions:

Yes ☐   No ☐

// CLAIRE'S CHIROPRACTIC: WORKSHEET ANSWERS //

Target Audience Persona

Personal Info

Age: 48

Gender: Female

Marital Status: married

Ages of Children, if any:
3, all in their 20s

Location: Portland, OR

Level of Education:
Master's degree

Occupation:
Retired RN, public speaker

Annual Income:
$120,000

Likes: spending time with her children, reading

Dislikes: sports

Challenges: overweight chronic pain

Role in the Purchase Process:
Hard to justify taking care of herself.
Main purchaser. No other people involved.

Goals: weight loss, increase walking, more travel

Values: feedback, knowledge, communication, hard work, flexibility

Words and ideas that appeal to this persona:
family, health, learning

Name

Lisa

Buying Habits

Shopping by percentage

In-store: 70% Online: 30%

Favorite places to buy:
Macy's, Barnes & Noble

How often do they buy:
twice a month

Relies on customer reviews:

Yes ☒ No ☐

Sorces of Info

Books/Magazines:
romance novels, self-help
Women's Health, Cosmo

Blogs: The Pioneer Woman, She Knows, Tiny Buddha, TED blog

Websites: Pinterest
Facebook

Television & Other Media:
Big Bang Theory, Game of Thrones, Shameless

Associations:
American Nurses Assn
American Chiro. Assn

Social Media Use

Favorite social media platforms:
Facebook
Pinterest

Frequency of social media use: daily

Uses social media to shape buying decisions:

Yes ☒ No ☐

TARGET AUDIENCE PERSONA

CHAPTER 3

Business Basics

Naming Your Business

If you've already got a name that works, that's fantastic. You may want to skim through this section quickly. If you're a start-up, or thinking of changing the name of your business (or may want to eventually), read on.

Choosing a name for your business can be a challenge — and fun. What you name your business should fit with the industry, it should be appealing to your target market, and it should give some hint at what your business does. Competition in your marketplace also plays a role.

Today's rules for naming businesses have changed, even in the last decade. While some tried-and-true rules apply, like keeping it short and easy to spell, the birth of search engine optimization has added a new element. You want a name that is unique and has as little virtual competition as possible (i.e. — when you Google your business name you want to show up on the first page).

The fun part comes when you sit down to brainstorm a preliminary list of ideas. You may end up with five, ten or more names on this list. Some will be more relevant than others. And you'll like some more than others, too. But jot down whatever ideas come to mind. Anything goes.

Then you'll work on paring down the list. Don't feel the need to rush this step. Visit and re-visit your list, eliminating some and keeping those with the most gut-instinct appeal. Ask others for their point of view, too. A name you think works may not have much logical reasoning to others. Arrive at your short list, which may have three to five good options.

Trusting your gut instincts here is smart, but there are also practical reasons why it's important to be scrupulous in the name you pick for your business.

Ask the following questions for each potential name on your short list.

- Does this name communicate what my business does?
- Does this name allow for future change and growth?

PRO TIP:

Save time with these online tools for domain and social media name usage:

At www.DomainsBot.com type in a keyword that you want to use in your potential website domain name and it will return a list of available domains.

With www.KnowEm.com you can check for the use of your desired name on over 500 social media sites.

- Does the name have a lot of competition when searched on Google?

- Will my target audience respond favorably to this name?

- Has any other company registered or trademarked this name?

- Is the name already taken as a website domain name on social media?

- Does this name have timeless appeal?

- Does this name have any negative connotation associated with it?

Once you've narrowed the list down to the final contenders, the choice really is up to you — it is your business after all. Pick the name that you truly believe in.

Our business owner, Claire, went through this exercise and realized her name wasn't encompassing all of the benefits offered by her business.

She learned a key element was missing in her business name and, therefore, updated it to **Claire's Chiropractic & Wellness Center**.

The new name more clearly defines that her business offers various therapies and products (like the massage and weight-loss coaching) in addition to chiropractic care.

Mission Statement

Every business has a Mission Statement, more or less. But what exactly is a Mission Statement? And do you really need one?

According to entrepreneur.com, a Mission Statement is,

> *"a sentence describing a company's function, markets and competitive advantages; a short written statement of your business goals and philosophies."*

And that's just it: a short written statement of your business goals and philosophies. A business's Mission Statement is an opportunity to define the company's culture, ethics, and goals for making decisions. It's important, but it doesn't have to be complicated. The best Mission Statements describe the goals of the business for its customers, employees, and owners. (And yes, you need one.)

There's no need to go about writing a Mission Statement alone. Here are a few steps to get you started:

1. If you've already completed your **Target Audience Persona Worksheet**, start there. It's important to have a distinct understanding of who your customer is and their buying preferences. Write down how your customer's life is better because your business exists.

2. Think about the value your brand delivers to your employees. Describe how your business is good for them.

3. Think about the impact your business has on you, the owner, as well as any other financial stakeholders. Is your goal to grow? In what way? Is it to have peace of mind about cash flow in order to enhance the principal owner's financial position? Or to break even while making the world a better place? Think it over and write it down.

4. Now, review what you've written so far. Mission Statements are usually just a sentence or two—or a short paragraph at the most—so it's important to be clear and concise. You should be able to express your objectives in several well-defined thoughts.

As a final test, does your Mission Statement answer all these questions?

a. What do you do? What do you stand for? And why do you do it?

b. What markets are you serving, and what benefits do you offer them?

c. Do you solve a problem for your customers?

d. Does it speak to the work environment you want for your employees?

For fun, here are examples of well-written Mission Statements from some well-known companies. What can you take away from them to help you craft your Mission Statement?

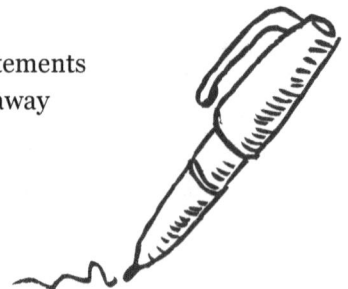

Disney

Be one of the world's leading producers and providers of entertainment and information. Using our portfolio of brands to differentiate our content, services and consumer products, we seek to develop the most creative, innovative and profitable entertainment experiences and related products in the world.

Louis Vuitton

Create products that embody unique savoir-faire, a carefully preserved heritage and a dynamic engagement with modernity. These creations make our Houses ambassadors of a distinctively redefined art de vivre.

Advance Auto Parts

It is the Mission of Advance Auto Parts to provide personal vehicle owners and enthusiasts with the vehicle related products and knowledge that fulfill their wants and needs at the right price. Our friendly, knowledgeable and professional staff will help inspire, educate and problem-solve for our customers.

Dole Food Company

Dole Food Company, Inc. is committed to supplying the consumer and our customers with the finest, high-quality products and to leading the industry in nutrition research and education. Dole supports these goals with a corporate philosophy of adhering to the highest ethical conduct in all its business dealings, treatment of its employees, and social and environmental policies.

For Claire's chiropractic business, her number one mission is to help her customers live more comfortably. She also desires to create a gratifying work environment for her small group of employees. With these ideas as her base, Claire's Mission Statement passes the final test questions.

Mission Statement for Claire's Chiropractic & Wellness Center

Claire's Chiropratic & Wellness Center improves the lives of its customers through innovative chiropractic technique and care. Our staff is committed to contributing to the total wellness of every customer, enabling them to live more comfortably.

CHAPTER 4

Brand Identity

You've learned a lot and gathered great information during your research and target audience analysis. You now know how others perceive you and your competitors, you've identified what you're best at, where you can improve and how you can build upon both, and you've discovered your ideal customer base. You've found the heart of your brand. With this information in your pocket, you can now formulate a distinguished brand that aligns with your business's mission and vision.

Now it's time for the fun stuff — the visual elements (or "brand identity") of your business! There are a lot of great businesses out there with bad logos. And there are bad businesses with great logos. You should strive to be great in all aspects of your business and have totally great visuals.

Your brand's logo will visually differentiate your business from its competitors. It has to be unique, depict your business brand, and appeal to the ideal customers outlined in your **Target Audience Persona Worksheets**.

> **A logo is an essential part of your brand identity as it becomes the mark by which consumers recognize your business.**

The tagline

Taglines are not required but can add clarity to what your brand offers and what makes it different. If you don't come up with a tagline from the start, don't worry, you can easily add one later. If you do have a tagline to incorporate, remember shorter is better. Ideally, ten syllables or less gives it that hook and makes it clearly recognizable.

Think about your favorite brands and their taglines:

> *"Just Do It"*
> *"Think Different"*
> *"Because You're Worth It"*
> *"Got Milk?"*
> *"Melts in Your Mouth, Not in Your Hands"*

What do they have in common? In a few words, they communicate a decisive attribute that's relevant and memorable.

To write your standout tagline, go back to your list of strengths. Use the positive attributes to write a slogan that tells people what makes you better than the competition. What makes you different? What benefit do you offer? What problem do you solve? What unique characteristic about your business is worth taking center stage? Tap into the creativity of your employees to develop the perfect tagline.

For our sample business, we opted to not include a tagline because we felt the addition of "& Wellness Center" to the business name effectively expressed the additional services available to Claire's patients.

Logo design

A logo is an essential part of your brand identity as it becomes the mark by which consumers recognize your business. As you begin thinking about the design of your business logo, it's important to have your target audience in mind. Be mindful to consider what your *market* wants, not what *you* personally like. You're not selling to yourself so be sure to develop your logo with your customer in mind.

Refer to your **Target Audience Persona Worksheets** to help you tailor your logo to your brand and target market.

With logo design, there are three fundamental elements: colors, fonts, and imagery. Let's look at each element and its role in your logo design.

> Colors

The world is full of color — we all have our favorites! Subconsciously, as consumers, we associate different colors with different meanings. Colors evoke feelings and affect our moods. That's why your brand color(s) choice is so important.

People have connections to different colors and those connections influence buying habits. The power of color psychology can help you shape your brand. Look at the consumer goods your target market already buys to see how other brands use color.

The infographic *The Psychology of Color* on pages 41-42, provided by Webpage FX (find the original here: http://www.webpagefx.com/blog/web-design/psychology-of-color-infographic/), shows the characteristics of individual colors and how primary and secondary colors influence our buying behaviors.

Another thing to keep in mind when selecting colors: more complex colors, and multiple colors, can increase printing costs. To keep printing production costs down, it's wise to select no more than two basic colors for a logo design. Two colors are simplest to work with for you and make it easier for your audience to recognize and remember your brand.

For Claire's Chiropractic's new logo, we chose eggplant and soft coral hues. Both colors are warm and inviting, the feelings Claire wants customers to feel upon visiting her practice.

#680e2d

#fc9565

> Font choice

Choosing a font for a business or brand logo may seem like no big deal — just pick one and get on with it. Not so fast.

Fonts speak volumes about the vibe, perception and overall aesthetic of a brand. You want to choose your font(s), also called "typeface," with purpose.

There are thousands of fonts out there, so being thoughtful and selective about font choice can be quite the daunting task. But don't fret. Here are some important tips to help you select the right font for your brand:

- Choose a font that visually describes the voice of your product and service. A script font won't pair well with an auto care business, and likewise, a grungy typeface may not be the best representation of an in-home daycare. Let common sense guide you.

- Serif typefaces (the ones with the little "feet") are classic and traditional. Sans-serif typefaces (those with streamlined letters) are contemporary and modern. Let the tone and personality of your brand determine which style of typeface fits best.

- Don't play it too safe. There are literally thousands of fonts out there. Do not pick Arial or Times

PRO TIP:

Choose a few adjectives that describe your business (go to your **Look In The Mirror Worksheet**) and enter them at MyFonts.com to get some starter ideas.

New Roman or Calibri (and a few other 'nono's' we list below) — they're too plain and common. Your business deserves something better. You want it to have an impact.

- When we say your brand deserves a better font, we don't mean the most outlandish font you find. There's much to be said for classic, timeless fonts. There are hundreds of beautiful fonts. Again, it's about matching the brand's vibe with an appropriate font.

- Most of the time, one font will do. You may be chomping at the bit to add a second font for a tagline. A good and simple rule to follow is: keep it exactly the same, or change it a lot. If using a second font makes sense for your brand, choose something very different than the first typeface.

- Avoid these fonts. We still see people using the fonts on the 'no-no' list. They are overused. They offer your brand no originality. Please, for the love of Pete, do not use these fonts in your logo design:

Times New Roman	*Arial*
Comic Sans	*Papyrus*
Impact	*Copperplate*
Brush Script	*Courier*

For Claire's chiropractic business, we chose one font with modern appeal and used variations (light, regular and bold) of that font family. Our business name is scripted in the font **Montserrat**, a typeface that evokes a modern, clean appeal.

The second line was written in the light variation of the font for a clean, classic feel.

> Imagery

Most logos include some sort of imagery, often in the form of an icon. This is widely encouraged by marketing professionals and designers. An icon gives identity to a brand.

While there are some amazing brands out there that skipped the use of a graphical image (largely because the brand font is custom created, and hence, has an originality all its own), the icon of a brand often becomes its identity: think Apple®, McDonalds®, Nike®, Pepsi®, to name a few well-known brands.

Using an icon in your logo also gives variety to how you can visually represent your brand. The icon alone can be used to represent and strengthen your brand identity.

Like choosing a font, there are considerations to take into account when selecting graphical elements for your logo:

PRO TIP:

Back away from the free clipart! It may be tempting to go for the freebies, but you get what you pay for. Clipart is overused and is low quality. You won't be able to manipulate the image for signage or other graphics. We can't think of a single good reason to use free clipart. There are stock photo websites with great vector images where you'll find the perfect image to match your brand. You'll have to pay a small price for it, but it's well worth it.

- Choose an icon with timeless appeal. Ask yourself if the image will still be relevant five or ten years from now.

- Choose an icon that appropriately demonstrates the image and values you've set forth for your brand and business.

- Choose an icon that will resonate with your audience.

- Keep it clean. Be sure nothing about the icon can be construed as inappropriate on any level.

The circle elements in the logo for Claire's Chiropractic & Wellness Center symbolize the wholistic approach to wellness and visually represent the shape of the spine.

CLAIRE'S CHIROPRACTIC
& WELLNESS CENTER

Putting it Together

Once you've chosen the perfect font, picked the best colors and selected an icon that is the perfect representation for your brand, it's time to marry them together to create your logo.

If you have the resource of a designer-friend, they may be willing to give you a few tips on how to put the two together for a top-notch logo. If you're all on your own, don't worry, you can do it!

Here are a few things to consider as you create your logo:

- Try multiple looks. Maybe the icon goes better on top of the wording, or maybe it looks better to the side. Maybe you prefer the look of the icon in color and words in black. Or maybe just the opposite.

  Play with a variety of options and then present them to some close friends or family to get their input. Like anything else, sometimes, if you're too close to it, it can be hard to form an objective opinion.

- Logos are usually designed in both horizontal and vertical versions, for use across different applications.

  For instance, a Facebook profile photo will use a vertical application of your logo, whereas a logo on printed letterhead may work better in a horizontal layout. Having both options isn't required, but it allows your logo to be used in multiple formats and sizes.

- First design your logo in color, but also create an all-black version and an all-white version. Additionally, you'll want a version with a transparent background.

PRO TIP:

A favicon (short for "favorite icon") is a small image associated with your website. It's 16x16 pixels and appears in the address bar or bookmark page of a browser. Create a favicon while you're working on your logo and add it to your website later. There are also a number of online tools, such as www.favicon.cc, that will help you develop the image. Remember to keep your branding consistent, even at such a small size!

- With all of these options, you'll be ready to apply your logo to any medium.

BONUS: Look Like a Pro with Brand Guidelines

Once your logo has been finalized, you should create a Brand Guidelines (sometimes called "Logo Identity Guidelines") document. Brand Guidelines are a simple set of rules on how your brand — including the name and logo — is allowed to be used. It includes the font (and its variations, such as bold and italics), the colors of the logo, the background colors you allow the logo to be printed atop and how much space should be allowed around your logo in print design.

Most brands have a set of Brand Guidelines. Even if you're just getting your company started, having guidelines established will ensure consistency in your branding and set a good precedent for moving your business forward.

Don't stress about this. You don't need to have a complex 20-page document to impress. Start with a simple document to record the information.

1. Open any word processing software and start a new document.

2. Log the fonts/typefaces you use. Indicate which parts of the name and logo use which fonts (if more than one is used).

3. Note your brand's official colors. Colors have color values, like RGB, CMYK and hex values, for use on the web. We recommend writing down the values for each type.

4. Note any sources of photography, so you know where to find more of a style you've used in the past.

5. List the file name for your official logo, and where it can be found on your computer.

6. Your Brand Guidelines should be a working document. Continue adding to the document as you make new or improved design decisions.

We've created two Brand Guidelines documents for Claire's business. The first version follows our instructions for creating a simple Brand Guidelines document.

The second, as shown on page 38, is a more artistic approach that contains additional elements. It is in line with what you would expect to receive from a marketing agency or creative designer.

Brand Guidelines — Sample

Logo:

CLAIRE'S CHIROPRACTIC
& WELLNESS CENTER

Fonts: Montserrat font family
Claire's: Monterrat Light
Chiropractic: Montserrat Bold
& Wellness Center: Montserrat Regular

Colors and color values:

Primary
Deep purple: C39 M98 Y64 K47; R104 G14 B45; #680e2d
Coral: C0 M51 Y63 K0; R252 G149 B101; #fc9565

Secondary
Dusty lavendar: C37 M68 Y41 K8; R157 G98 B114; #9d6272
Pale lavendar: C15 M26 Y15 K0; R213 G187 B194; # d5bbc2

Logo file location: [file path]

CLAIRE'S CHIROPRACTIC BRAND GUIDELINES

PRIMARY LOGO

REVERSE MONOCHROME LOGO

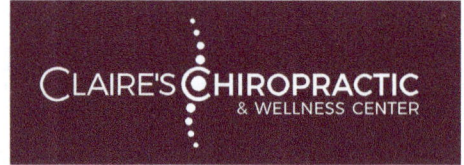

FAVICONS

LOGO TYPOGRAPHY

Montserrat

ABCDEFGHIJKLMNOPQRSTUVWXYZ
abcdefghijklmnopqrstuvwxyz
0123456789

Montserrat / Light

Montserrat / Bold

Montserrat / Regular

LOGO COLORS

#680c2d   #fc9366   #9e6072

SECONDARY BRAND COLORS

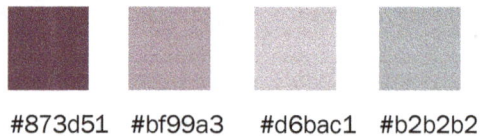

#873d51   #bf99a3   #d6bac1   #b2b2b2

STYLE GUIDE

Website design and usability

Aside from the product itself, a website is the most visible element of a brand's identity. Think about your own information gathering and prospective buying habits. Where do you turn first when you want to learn about a business, find out about the benefits of any given product or where to buy something? The internet, of course. And your target audience behaves in the same way.

Prospective customers will look you up online, so the information presented on your website plays a significant role in creating your brand identity and building visitor engagement. A website is often the first impression of a business to the public, so conveying the benefits that one will experience by doing business with you are critical.

A website is often the first impression of a business to the public.

There's a lot more to website planning and building than we present here, but it's helpful to recognize how branding is woven into every aspect of what you do, and your online presence a key piece.

> Color Scheme

As you learned earlier in this chapter on logo design, colors aren't just about aesthetics — they evoke emotions and subconscious associations. They set a mood.

In most cases, it's wise to use the same color palette as you used in your logo to reinforce your overall branding. You can play up the secondary colors you outlined in your Brand Guidelines with elements like buttons, sidebars and calls to action (Call to Action, or CTA, is an instruction to the audience to get an immediate response, such as "Call Now", "Click Here" and "Buy Today").

Be sure to maintain consistency. There should be a consistent visual color connection between your logo and your website.

> Emotion & Tone

The words on the pages of your website are your opportunities to speak directly to your customers and prospective buyers. What emotion do you want visitors to experience when perusing your site? What attitudes do you want them to associate with your brand? Is your tone friendly and down to earth, or more formal?

This is another instance where your research will come in handy. Use your **Look in the Mirror Worksheet** for ideas, and match the vibe you outlined there in the tone of your website.

PRO TIP:

When creating contact forms on your website, use fields that capture important Persona data. For example, if your different Personas vary based on company size, add a field to your contact form that asks for company size. The information you gather can help you further refine your Target Audience Persona Worksheets.

> Overall Design & Layout

Whether your site visitors realize it or not, the design and layout of your website are critical elements of your website's usability (the ease of use for the visitor) and thus, how they interact with you in a digital space.

Today's websites are big, bold and utilize clean design tactics. Adding fun and interactive elements can be a risk worth taking, if it makes sense for your business, but they can also distract from the message you're trying to convey and action you want your visitors to take.

Our top three recommendations for layout and overall design are:

1. Keep your design and layouts consistent from page to page and device to device. Your site must carry your brand no matter the size of the screen it's being used on.

2. Use simple navigation, including placing your logo to the upper left space on every page, linking back to the site's home page.

3. Utilize clear and engaging calls-to-action.

PSYCHOLOGY
OF COLOR

84.7% of consumers cite color as the primary reason they buy a particular product.

WHEN PEOPLE BUY

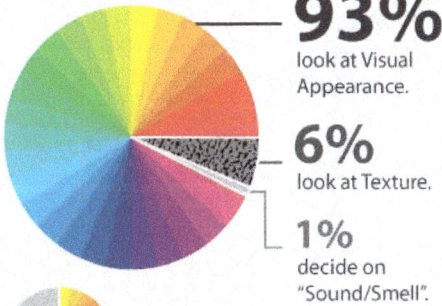

93% look at Visual Appearance.

6% look at Texture.

1% decide on "Sound/Smell".

80% think color increases brand recognition.

"Research reveals people make a sub-conscious judgment about an environment or product within **90 seconds** of initial viewing. Between **62%** and **90%** of that assessment is based on color alone."

90s

52% of shoppers did not return to a store due to overall aesthetics.

OUTCOME OF THE USE OF COLOR

Ads in color are read up to

42% more often

than the same ads **in black and white.**

COLOR CAN IMPROVE

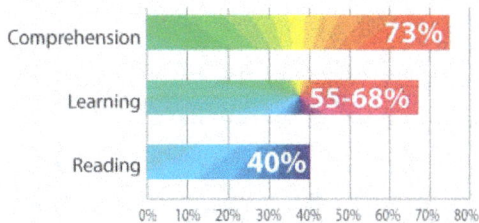

Comprehension	**73%**
Learning	**55-68%**
Reading	**40%**

0% 10% 20% 30% 40% 50% 60% 70% 80%

PRIMARY COLORS

SECONDARY COLORS

RED YELLOW BLUE ORANGE GREEN PURPLE

RED
PRIMARY COLOR

PERSONALITY/EMOTIONS
- Evokes strong emotions
- Encourages appetite
- Increases passion and intensity
- Red roses symbolize love

MARKETING
- Increases heart rate
- Used by restaurants to stimulate appetite
- Creates urgency often seen in clearance sales
- Used for impulsive shoppers

POLITICS
- Represents Communist or Socialist parties worldwide
- Used for Republicans in the USA

CHAKRA
Root chakra
- Located at base of the spine
- Related to survival, safety, physical self

COMPANIES

ORANGE
SECONDARY COLOR

PERSONALITY/EMOTIONS
- Reflects excitement, enthusiasm
- Shows warmth
- Warns of caution

MARKETING
- Signifies aggression
- Creates call to action: Buy, Sell, Subscribe
- Found in impulsive shoppers
- Represent a friendly, cheerful, confident brand

POLITICS
- Orange is the national color of the Netherlands and its royal family

CHAKRA
The Sacral chakra
- Located around lower back and reproductive organs
- Related to sexuality, creativity, pleasure

COMPANIES

YELLOW
PRIMARY COLOR

PERSONALITY/EMOTIONS
- Increases cheerfulness, warmth
- Causes fatigue and strain on the eyes
- Makes babies cry
- Stimulates mental processes
- Stimulates nervous system
- Encourages communication

MARKETING
- Represents optimism, youthfulness
- Used to grab attention of window shoppers
- Shows clarity

POLITICS
- Represents Liberalism

CHAKRA
Solar Plexus chakra
- Located in upper abdomen between navel and sternum
- Related to personal power, will, self esteem

COMPANIES

GREEN
SECONDARY COLOR

PERSONALITY/EMOTIONS
- Constitutes health, tranquility
- Symbolizes money
- Denotes nature
- Alleviates depression
- Workers in a green environment have fewer stomach aches
- Green is used in night vision goggles because the human eye is most sensitive to and able to discern the most shades of it
- Represents new growth

MARKETING
- Used to relax in stores
- Associated with wealthy
- Green M&M's are said to send a sexual message
- Has long been a symbol of fertility
- Was once the preferred color choice for wedding gowns in the 15th century

POLITICS
- Connected to Environmentalists

CHAKRA
Heart chakra
- Center of body, heart level
- Related to unconditional love, healing

COMPANIES

BLUE
PRIMARY COLOR

PERSONALITY/EMOTIONS
- Associated with water, peace
- Most preferred by men
- Represent calmness or serenity
- Curbs appetite
- Known as a "cold" color
- Perceived as constant in human life due to sky and ocean being blue
- Increases productivity
- Most used color for offices

MARKETING
- Often used in corporate business because it's productive and non-invasive
- Creates sense of security and trust in a brand

POLITICS
- Represents Conservative parties worldwide
- Used for Democrats in the USA

CHAKRA
Throat chakra
- Base of throat
- Related to communication, truth, self-expression

COMPANIES

PURPLE
SECONDARY COLOR

PERSONALITY/EMOTIONS
- Showed royalty, wealth, success, wisdom
- Many kings wore purple robes

MARKETING
- Used often in beauty or anti-aging products
- Used to soothe or calm
- Represent a creative, imaginative, wise brand

POLITICS
- Used for royalty, but hardly used in modern politics

CHAKRA
The Crown chakra
- Top of the head
- Related to spiritual life and experience, connection to the divine, pure consciousness, transcendence

COMPANIES

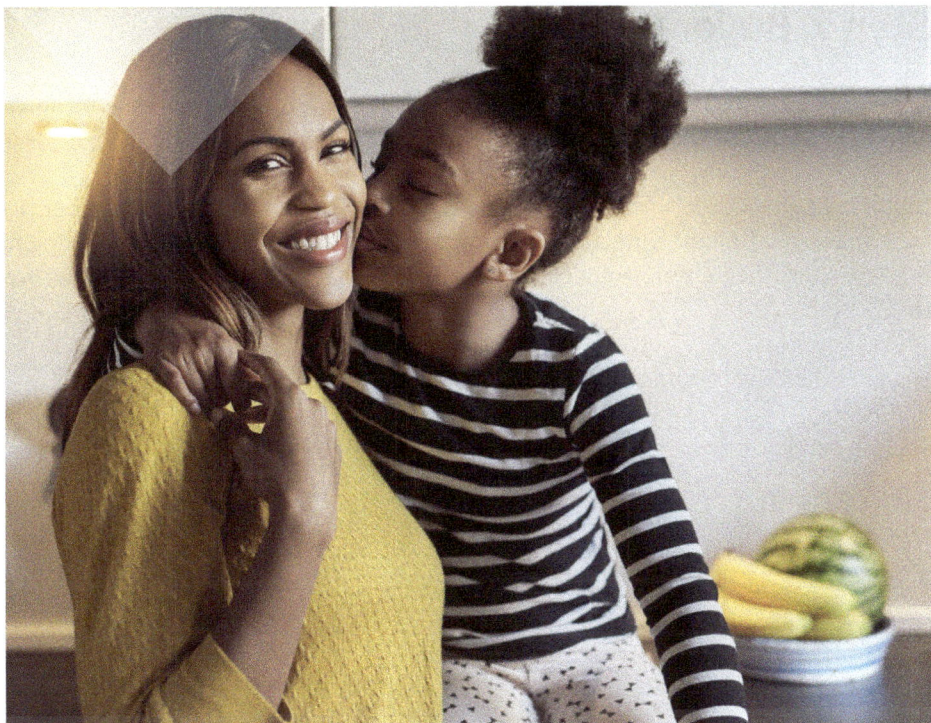

CHAPTER 5

BONUS: Step-by-Step Guide to Targeted Marketing Copy

In this bonus chapter we guide you, step-by-step, to create message points that you can use to reach and attract your audience. The concepts you've learned, and the work you've done thus far, will help you along the way.

Note: Intermediate-level concepts ahead! (You're ready for it!)

Step 1. Buyer Profiles

With your primary **Target Audience Persona** in hand, we'll now consider some "Buyer Profiles" for that Persona.

In our example, Claire's primary Persona is a 45-year-old woman who experiences back pain. Who might purchase a chiropractic visit for her: the woman herself, her husband, her employer, a close friend? These are the Buyer Profiles for this Persona.

Who are the Buyer Profiles for your primary Target Audience Persona?

Jot down at least two:

1. _____

2. _____

3. _____

4. _____

5. _____

Step 2. What is the hook?

As consumers, we make purchases based on the perceived or promised outcome: "How will I benefit from this purchase?" and "What problem will this product/ service solve for me?" We buy outcomes. We buy with anticipation of the "after-state" that we will experience by having and using the product or service.

In this step, using the **What's the Hook Worksheet** provided on pg 47, you'll write down the before-state and after-state that someone could experience when using your product or service. Not every prompt will apply to your product or service. Pick those that make the most sense for you.

We've provided some examples for Claire's Chiropractic to help.

Word prompt: *have*

What does someone have now?
What will they have after they buy?

Claire's customers have back pain now; after they receive her services they have reduced or eliminated their back pain.

Word prompt: *feel*

What does the consumer feel now?
What might they feel after?

For Claire's customers, they feel uncomfortable, defeated; after they feel relief and hope.

Word prompt: *average day*

How can your product/service affect the average day of your customer?

Claire's customers will experience a more productive day with the ability to move without back pain.

Word prompt: *status*

Does your product elevate your customer's status or professional position?

This prompt isn't relevant for Claire, but it might be for you.

Word prompt: *proof or results*

Customers who experience positive results from using your product or service may be willing to give you a results-based testimonial. Testimonials are statements of your customers' experiences and recommendations that are a valuable form of word-of-mouth-marketing.

This prompt isn't relevant for Claire, but it might be for you.

Word prompt: *speed and automation*

Will using your product or service help your customer simplify their life in some way? Will it make completing tasks quicker and easier? What are the before and after processes in relation to using your product/service?

This prompt isn't relevant for Claire, but it might be for you.

Step 3. Create messaging for each Buyer Profile.

With the **What's the Hook? Worksheet** completed, next, you'll use the **Targeted Messaging Points Worksheet** to help you hone in on messaging points for your Buyer Profiles. Add your Buyer Profiles from Step 1 to the top of the chart. Add your Hooks from Step 2 to the left of the chart.

Now it's time to put on your creative thinking cap. Use the chart to plot key messaging points for each Buyer Profile and Hook combination. You want each Buyer to know "what's in it for them?" when they buy from you.

In our example, we have a 45-year-old woman as our Buyer Profile and a desired after-state of being pain free. Our messaging point for our "pain free" hook is simply *"You don't have to live with back pain."* For our next Buyer Profile, the woman's husband, we used *"What if we told you we can ease your wife's back pain?"* And for our third Buyer Profile, the employer, we chose *"If Lisa didn't have back pain, she'd be happier (and more productive) at work."*

Use words and ideas from the **Target Audience Persona Worksheet** to zero in on phrases that will appeal to this Persona and the associated buyer profiles.

Step 4: Use these messaging points in advertising, social media posts, and other marketing avenues.

The messaging points are ideal for Social Media but the concepts can be used anywhere.

Take it one step at a time. Practice this concept with your primary Target Audience Persona and relevant Buyer Profiles. Once you've developed messaging points that you feel will resonate with this group, you can use this approach to fine-tune messaging for all of your Personas.

BONUS Step-by-Step Guide to Targeted Marketing Copy

WHAT'S THE HOOK?	BEFORE-STATE	AFTER-STATE
Have		
Feel		
Average Day		
Status		
Proof / Results		
Speed / Automation		

BONUS Step-by-Step Guide to Targeted Marketing Copy

TARGETED MESSAGING POINTS

	BUYER PROFILES		
	BUYER PROFILE A	BUYER PROFILE B	BUYER PROFILE C
HOOK 1			
HOOK 2			
HOOK 3			
HOOK 4			
HOOK 5			

HOOKS

BONUS Step-by-Step Guide to Targeted Marketing Copy

STEP-BY-STEP GUIDE TO TARGETED MARKETING COPY. WHAT'S THE HOOK?

// CLAIRE'S CHIROPRACTIC: WORKSHEET ANSWERS //

WHAT'S THE HOOK?

	BEFORE-STATE	AFTER-STATE
Have	back pain	pain relief or pain free
Feel	back pain	pain relief / hope for living without pain
Average Day	Most days include living with pain, slowing down activities, affecting mood and motivation	More productive days with the ability to move without back pain
Status	N/A	N/A
Proof / Results	N/A	customer testimonials
Speed / Automation	back pain slows down many daily functions	customers will be more productive, able to complete daily tasks more quickly w/o pain

BONUS Step-by-Step Guide to Targeted Marketing Copy

TARGETED MESSAGING POINTS

BUYER PROFILES

HOOKS		BUYER PROFILE A 45-YEAR-OLD WOMAN	BUYER PROFILE B WOMAN'S HUSBAND	BUYER PROFILE C WOMAN'S EMPLOYER
HOOK 1	Pain free	You don't have to live with back pain.	What if we told you we can ease your wife's back pain?	If Lisa didn't have back pain, she'd be happier (and more productive) at work.
HOOK 2	Relief & hope	This is the relief you've been looking for.	Relief comes in many forms when you're not in pain.	
HOOK 3	Testimonial	Dr. Claire changed my life.	When someone you love is free of pain it means the world. I can't thank Dr. Claire enough for what she's done for my wife.	
HOOK 4				
HOOK 5				

CHAPTER 6

Expanding Your Reach

With a well-defined brand, you're set to start your marketing initiatives and get the word out about your business. Next, we offer some advertising insights:

> Be consistent

Have you heard this mantra before: "Consistency is Key." It wholeheartedly applies in advertising. The messages you deliver to communicate your brand should be consistent across all avenues. Develop a marketing approach that includes clear and concise messaging and run with it.

> Spot check

Is someone on your team a bit on the OCD side? Very detail-oriented? Assign that person to review your marketing and advertising pieces. This is where those Brand Guidelines will come in handy.

In the hustle and bustle of business, it's helpful to have that second (or even third) set of eyes to help ensure consistency. After working on something for a while, it's easy to miss a detail that will jump out for someone new to the material.

> Share your expertise

In marketing, we suggest using the 80/20 rule. It says the content you publish should offer your customers (and potential customers) 80% in educational materials and 20% sales information.

This holds especially true in social media marketing.

Your audience will actively engage with your brand when they see you as an expert, someone who provides and shares information that will help them solve problems, not just pushing a "buy now" message. Educational and informative pieces can certainly include a soft sale — how you can help them — but keep the messaging simple and near the end of the piece.

Thanks to your **Target Audience Persona Worksheet**, you know where your customers are spending their time online. Use the bonus **Social Media 101 Checklist** on page 53 to help you initiate your social media presence.

BONUS: Social Media 101 Checklist

☐ **Pick the social media networks that make the best sense for your business.**

Ask this question: Where does your target audience "hang out" online? Use the **Target Audience Persona Worksheets** to guide you. Check out this list for additional help:

Teenagers: Vine, Snapchat, YouTube, Tumblr, Instagram

Engaged and Expectant Mothers: Pinterest

People under 50 with a college education: Twitter

Women, young adults 18-29: Instagram

Women, young parents and grandparents: Facebook

College graduates, higher income houses: LinkedIn

Bloggers and influencers: Twitter, Tumblr

☐ **Decide on one name to use across all social media networks. Keep it consistent.**

My social media moniker: _____

☐ **Determine your primary purpose for being on social media:**

Brand awareness? Clicks through to your website? Growing your contact list? Educating your audience?

Choose a goal and move through the remaining steps with that in mind.

☐ **Set up your accounts.**

Starting with your first social media network, follow the site's steps to create your business profile. Add plenty of detail while keeping it clear and concise. Potential customers who want to find out about you will look to your social media accounts for information. Use these spaces to tell them why you're the right choice for their business.

Stay true to your branding. Use profile photos and graphics that sync with the look and feel established in your Brand Guidelines.

PRO TIP: Less is more when it comes to your social media accounts. You don't want to find yourself overwhelmed, which can happen if you're active on every platform. Abandoned accounts give the impression of carelessness and lack of follow-through. To keep that from happening to you, focus on one social media site to start.

BONUS: Social Media 101 Checklist

☐ **Prepare your content.**

Content marketing (a strategic marketing approach focused on creating and distributing content) has become a huge part of how businesses connect with their audience.

Social media is about sharing great content. Reuse blog posts, press releases and lifestyle shots from your website. Think about how you can take one piece of content and re-purpose it across many different platforms and in different ways. Your content goal should be to provide value!

☐ **Network.**

Follow brand influencers, experts, marketers, companies and industry publications. Spend 10-15 minutes a day studying, learning and interacting with them. Share their posts on your social media sites!

☐ **Get the word out.**

Make it easy for people to find you on social media. Add links and icons for your social media accounts to everything: your website, business cards, email signature and every piece of advertising. Notify your contacts and ask them to follow your social accounts.

☐ **Do the minimum to start. Then do more.**

Set a realistic goal for how often you will be active on your social sites. It's exciting as you get started and, likewise, easy to over-commit yourself with lofty goals of posting and sharing content. Follow these standards of what's "expected" on the most popular platforms and establish sensible goals for yourself: Start small and build from there.

Website blog: post once a week
Facebook, Instagram, LinkedIn, Vine: post 3x/week
Tweet: post 10x/week
Pin: post 20x/week

PRO TIP: Use Canva or PicMonkey to update and edit photos on your social media accounts. You can also download free stock photos from LifeofPix.com.

CHAPTER 7

Creating an Oustanding Customer Experience

In Chapter One, we said branding starts at the top of an organization and permeates through the ranks. We can't stress this enough. Branding success takes clear direction on how you wish and expect your brand be communicated in all aspects of the business.

Your employees are the face of your business. It's imperative they understand and embrace your vision. Don't assume your employees understand the mission and

Employees who feel empowered will serve you (and your brand) well!

vision of your brand. It's your job to educate them, and to get them excited to be your brand ambassadors. The success of your business relies on the customer experience you create and deliver.

Use these tips to build an outstanding customer experience through employees who are informed, engaged and empowered to deliver your brand.

> Informed

Customer interaction is another opportunity for your business to share its brand directly with the consumer. Develop a training program for your employees that includes a review of your branding elements. Encourage other employees to serve as mentors to newbies who come aboard. Train with examples — both good and bad — of how you expect customer-related situations be handled. Ensure everyone knows how to interact with customers. Devise the lingo you want employees to use when speaking to customers. When it comes to customer interactions, don't give employees the opportunity to "wing it."

> Engaged

Rewards systems that honor awesome interactions and brand reinforcement are great at keeping employees engaged. Simple thank you notes, treats or a free lunch go a long way to show appreciation, and are likely to encourage future positive behaviors.

> Empowered

Listen to your employees' feedback and act on what they say. While not every idea will be a good one, nor every complaint legitimate, give every matter brought to you by an employee careful consideration. It's your responsibility as an employer, and it empowers your employees to feel their ideas, opinions and concerns matter.

Employees who feel empowered will serve you (and your brand) well!

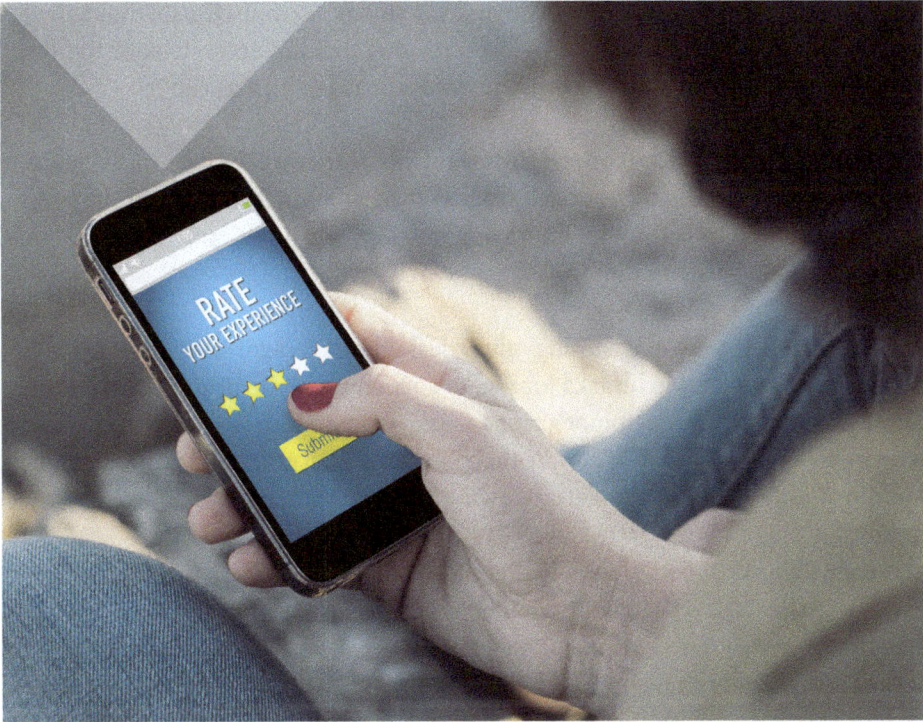

CHAPTER 8

Keep Your Eye on Your Brand

As days course on and you tend to your day-to-day operations, it's important to stay attentive to the reputation your brand has earned through customer interactions.

Customer reviews have become a popular way to rate products and services. They're one of best ways to gauge how customers perceive your business across different facets, including the product or service you offer, your timeliness and customer service. And they're a key factor in driving future business.

Consumers love to research before buying, and today's online climate makes it very easy. Like it or not, your business will get reviews that are accessible for the world to read. You want to make sure those reviews are as positive as can be!

We've put together a **Customer Satisfaction Survey** template on page 59 to help you gather firsthand feedback from your customers. You'll glean important information to help you make improvements and you'll probably get a few good testimonials to use along that way.

Always remember, if a customer gives less-than-average scores on a survey, expresses dissatisfaction or asks for you to contact them, be prompt in your reply. Never let a dissatisfied customer's response go unanswered. Dissatisfied customers are inevitable. It's your job to handle their concerns with grace and professionalism. And on the flip side, if you get a glowing review from a customer, go the extra mile and reach out to them with a short note thanking them for their positive feedback and their continued business.

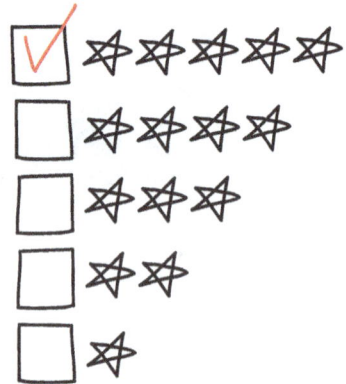

Customer Satisfaction Survey

Whether you send them digitally or in paper form, these questions will help you gather first-hand feedback from your customers.

Dear [Customer Name],

Thank you for giving [Business Name] the opportunity to serve you! Please take a few minutes to share your experience doing business with us. Your answers will help us know what we're doing well and identify areas where we can improve. Once you complete your survey you'll earn a coupon for [XX]% off your next purchase.

We look forward to serving you again,
[Owner's Name]
[Title], [Business Name]

1. Overall, how satisfied are you with [Product or Business Name]?
- Extremely Satisfied
- Somewhat Satisfied
- Neutral
- Somewhat Unsatisfied
- Extremely Unsatisfied

2. How likely are you to use/purchase [Product] again?
- Definitely will
- Probably will
- Might or might not
- Probably won't
- Definitely won't
- Never used

3. Were you treated in a professional and courteous manner by our staff?

Yes   No   N/A

4. Would you recommend [Product or Business Name] to others?
- Definitely would
- Probably would
- Might or might not
- Probably would not
- Definitely would not
- N/A

5. Please tell us about your experience with [Product or Business Name]. Your responses will help us to better serve you and may be used for employee training or marketing initiatives.

_____

_____

_____

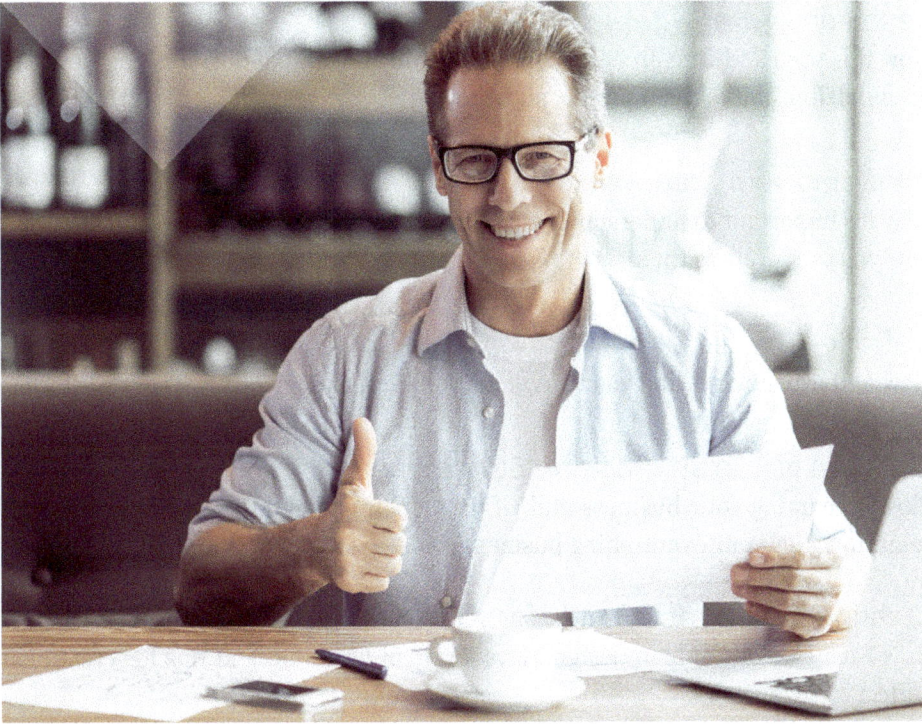

CHAPTER 9

Summing it Up

W e've reached the end of our guide. We covered a lot! Whether you're a marketing novice and this is entirely new material to you, or you have some working experience with the concepts we presented, it's a lot to digest. Let's review what you learned:

The basics of branding
How consumers identify with brands and use their feelings to shape their buying decisions.

Research
How this tried and true process helps you define the kind of business you desire to be and define and target a perfect audience.

Analyzing your competition
Why it's important to understand your competitors' strengths and weaknesses and how you can leverage them.

Defining your target market
How and why pinpointing your target market is crucial to your marketing efforts.

Business Name and Mission Statement
Tips for naming your business and writing a compelling Mission Statement that communicates your overarching business goals.

Creating the perfect visuals for your brand
How each element of logo design plays a role in branding and tips for creating a perfect company logo.

Website design
The elements of engaging website design that drive a positive user experience.

Expanding your reach
We offered insights to spark your advertising and marketing initiatives.

Creating an outstanding customer experience
How informing, engaging and empowering your employees sets the stage for happy, repeat customers.

Getting customer feedback
Why this post-sale activity helps you measure success.

Our hope is that this tutorial gives you the straight-forward, organized guidance you need to tackle each piece with confidence and a bit of ease. We wish you the very best of luck as you embark on your branding — or rebranding — journey!

A Hand to Help You Create an Awesome Brand

In running a business, branding is an essential piece of the puzzle that can easily be overlooked or forgotten altogether. If at any point, as you move through the steps outlined in this book, you're unsure how to move forward, or simply don't have the time to commit, that's OK! No one expects you to drop everything and become a branding expert.

Fresh Dezigns has been helping businesses like yours find their voice since 2008. Here are some of Fresh Dezigns' services:

Branding

We'll collaborate with you to create a brand that reflects everything you are as a business and helps you can stand out in the marketplace.

Graphic Design

Our graphic designers will give your brand a visual identity that perfectly encompasses your business's mission.

Web Design

Our web team will guide you to create an attractive and effective website to achieve your online marketing goals, whether to serve as an information hub or to boost online conversions, all while staying consistent to your branding.

Digital Marketing

Take your brand to the streets! Our digital marketing team works to increase your conversions, repeat traffic and online visibility through search engine optimization, pay-per-click marketing, funnel strategies, email marketing, social media marketing and social media advertising.

Let us make your branding and marketing journey as easy as possible. Contact us today to start your no-obligation consultation with our experienced brand developer.

Check out www.freshdezigns.com for more information.

Download the worksheets from the book at www.simplebusinessbranding.com.

Glossary of Marketing Terms

After-State: What the consumer will experience by having and using the product or service.

Before-State: What the consumer is experiencing prior to having and using the product or service.

Brand Audit: An examination of a business's current effectiveness and position in the marketplace based on perception of the brand.

Brand Guidelines: A simple set of rules on how your brand is allowed to be used. (also, Logo Identity Guidelines)

Brand Identity: The visual elements of your business that express how it wants to be perceived by consumers – name, tone, tagline, logos, colors, font, imagery.

Branding: The process involved in creating a unique name and image for a product in the consumer's mind, mainly through advertising campaigns with a consistent theme. Branding aims to establish a significant and differentiated presence in the market that attract and retains loyal customers. (www.businessdictionary.com)

Buyer Profile: A description of an individual who would purchase your product or service for themselves or for your Target Audience Persona.

Call to Action (CTA): An instruction to the audience to get an immediate response, such as "Call Now".

CMYK: A colour model that describes a color in terms of the quantity of each secondary colour (cyan, magenta, yellow), and "key" (black) it contains. The CMYK system is used for printing.

Content Marketing: A strategic marketing approach focused on creating and distributing valuable, relevant and consistent content to attract and retain your target market audience and ultimately drive them to purchase.

Demographic: A market segment with several shared traits, including age, race, gender, marital status, income, education and occupation.

Email Service Provider (ESP): A company that offers email marketing or bulk email services.

Favicon (favorite icon): A small image, 16x16 pixels, associated with your website that appears in the address bar or bookmark page of a browser.

Font: A particular size, weight and style of a typeface.

Hex Values: A way of specifying color using hexadecimal values. The code starts with a pound sign (#) and is followed by six hex values. The code is generally associated with HTML and websites or viewed on a screen.

Hook: Enticing offer, clever phrase or catchy jingle intended to capture the consumer's attention and speak to the target audience or buyer profile.

Icon: Logo imagery that gives identity to a brand.

Logo: A graphic mark, emblem or symbol used to promote and represent your business and brand.

Market Research: The process of gathering, analyzing and interpreting information about a market, product or service.

Mission Statement: A short written statement of your business goals and philosophies.

RGB (red, green, blue): A color model that adds red, green and blue ink together in various ways to reproduce colors.

Search Engine Results Page (SERP): The page displayed by a search engine after the user enters a keyword query.

Social Media Network: Forms of online communication through communities used to share idea, information and messages.

Social Media Moniker: A nickname used to define your online presence. (also, Social Media Handle)

Tagline: A catchphrase or slogan.

Target Audience: A particular group at which marketing is directed. (also, Ideal Target Audience, Ideal Customer)

Target Audience Persona: Fictional, generalized representations of your customers in visual form. (also, Persona)

Targeted Marketing Copy: Messaging points used in advertising to attract your target audience.

URL (Uniform Resource Locator): A global address used to locate a website on the internet. (also, Web Address)

Vibe: The thoughts and feelings your business brand portrays.

About the Author

Chrissy Carpenter is a marketing fanatic and owner of Fresh Dezigns; a marketing firm specializing in combining branding, graphic design, website design and digital marketing to create the ultimate one-stop-shop for business owners who need a push in the right direction.

While just breaking through to "published" status, Chrissy's background in marketing consists of 10+ years of real-world experience coupled with endless hours of trainings. While she finds the most satisfaction in helping start-ups build and grow, her experience with large companies such as H&R Block, The National Rifle Association, "YUM" Corporation, Lockton Insurance Companies and Block Real Estate have given her the skills to assist a company of any size.

Ready to get some help with your marketing? Stop by freshdezigns.com and leave Chrissy a note.

www.ingramcontent.com/pod-product-compliance
Lightning Source LLC
Chambersburg PA
CBHW081110220326
41598CB00038B/7305